WHY

RHODE

ISLAND

MATTERS!

First in Independence, Industry, Art & Innovation

ANN MARIE MARSHALL

Why Rhode Island Matters!
First in Independence, Industry, Art & Innovation
Special Limited 1st Edition

©2010, 2012, 2014 by Ann Marie Marshall

Check out the blog for updates:
http://whyrimatters.blogspot.com

This is the first imprint in a new series
SHORT ATTENTION SPAN BOOKS™
Quick reads for busy people™

An Imprint of
SHORELINE PRESS
P.O. Box 110
Slocum, RI 02877

Manufactured in the United States of America

ISBN 978-1-887671-04-0

Volume discounts available for educators, businesses,
promotions, and tourism offices. Write for pricing.

First Edition—Third Printing [April 2014]

Rhode Island
Matters!

*And whereas…they have freely declared,
that it is much on their hearts…
to hold forth a lively experiment,
that a most flourishing civil state may stand…*

Excerpted from
THE ROYAL CHARTER
Petitioned By John Clarke
GRANTED BY KING CHARLES II
JULY 5, 1663

Why Rhode Island Matters!

Preface

Summer is coming! Everywhere I look I see good news/bad news.

Let me get the not-so-good-news out of the way because this book is all about the good and amazing people, places, and things that have characterized my home state of Rhode Island over the past 378 years.

The not-so-good-news is everywhere. The whole world appears to be in turmoil with the future less clear than perhaps at any time since the great depression in the uncertain days of the early 1930's. Sadly, the current economy is depressed, the federal government is spending money at a furious pace with no positive impact, and the outlook of business owners and consumers is discouragingly low.

Rhode Island has suffered more than most, with one of the country's three highest rates of unemployment, high business, personal and property tax rates, and an unnerving amount of unfunded public employee pensions that may dog our economy for years.

But I am not discouraged. I know that despite what else is going on anywhere in this world: *Rhode Island Matters!*

Rhode Island has always mattered. In the next few pages I'll share some highlights of Rhode Island's amazing history of leadership and first-mover status in religion, government, industry, business, art and innovation. I think you'll quickly see and understand that we can embrace this past record of accomplishments to lead our communities, our state, and our nation into a successful future. *I hope you'll join me!*

Why Rhode Island Matters!

A Brief Introduction

There are at least 300 (3,000?!) books about Rhode Island, all with more information and details than I could ever put in this short volume. I know because I've read so many of them. You'll find a short list of some of these great books tucked into the end pages if you'd like more detail, more stories, and more history.

But my purpose here was not to exhaust my favorite subject --- Rhode Island---but rather to briefly and quickly remind you and all my fellow Rhode Islanders why this state matters.

So many of us have forgotten the vision, progress and amazing things that have taken place during our state's long and unique past. We have forgotten this is a great place with an illustrious history of great people who arrived here with little more than their spirit, their ideas, and their desire for freedom and for a place to worship, create, and live in peace, as they pleased and as they believed God ordained.

Most of all, we have forgotten that Rhode Island is a place where we can still make great things happen. And all of us can play a part because Rhode Island has something for everyone.

Rhode Island is a welcoming place for dreamers, inventors, builders, writers, musicians, and artists.

Why
Rhode Island
Matters!

Rhode Island is a resource rich place for sailors, fishermen, farmers, explorers, and scientists.

Rhode Island is an exciting and nurturing place for children, families, students, visitors, travelers, and tourists.

Rhode Island is a place with a rich history of independence, religious freedom, industrial development, transportation, education, mixing with a wonderful melting pot of many cultures, foods, and fashion.

With so much that is great already behind us, it seems that the future will be even better. I, too, believe it will.

Let us not long for the past, but embrace today and dream big dreams for tomorrow.

Amazingly, after more than 300 years of progress, the good old days are ahead of us.

Ann Marie Marshall
North Kingstown, RI
April 1, 2014

Why
Rhode Island
Matters!

What's With Our Name?

Though we have always been the nation's smallest state in square miles, our official state name has been the nation's longest. Our official name is **"The State of Rhode Island and Providence Plantations."**

Over the last couple hundred years there have been calls, some quiet, some less so, to change our name to something shorter, like "Rhode Island," and neatly snip off the balance of the state name. The reasons given vary, from a misnomer that the "Plantations" in our name somehow relates to slavery or some prior existence of farms (plantations) where slave labor was employed.

Rhode Island is the original and rightful name of what is known as Aquidneck Island (Newport). The use of the word "plantation" was an English word in those times of Rhode Island's Charter of 1663 that defined the act of men banding together to form a colony. The Charter banded together the towns of Portsmouth and Newport on Rhode Island together with the towns of Warwick and Providence (the Providence Plantations) to create Rhode Island and Providence Plantations.

Why
Rhode Island
Matters!

Rhode Island: Size Benchmark

We like being thought of for what we are---just the right size.

Our small size makes us the perfect target for writers and reporters seeking to describe something truly large compared to our modest 1,214 square miles. Many things have been compared to our state in order to help people envision the magnitude of the size and extent of some devastating event or natural disaster.

Recently I read the following descriptions:
"In the end, the massive wildfires in Southern California burned an area that many reports described as about the size of Rhode Island." (*Slate*, 2003) "The slick nearly tripled in just a day or so, growing from a spill the size of Rhode Island to something closer to the size of Puerto Rico…" (*Associated Press*, 2010)

Natural wonders have not been spared the comparison either.

Stephen Fried, in his 2010 book about Fred Harvey, *Appetite for America*, describes the size of the Grand Canyon: "It was more than a mile deep, and big enough to easily fit the state of Rhode Island, all five boroughs of New York City, and Washington, D.C."

In Mark Twain's 1907 "Captain Stormfield's Visit To Heaven," Twain describes the hereafter as, "a mean little ten-cent heaven about the size of Rhode Island."

Why
Rhode Island
Matters!

Our Maritime Heritage Continues

Everything Old is New Again

Not fa' nothin', but there's a reason we're known as the *Ocean State*.

Our maritime history stretches back to the earliest days of explorers who first reached these shores from Europe and can be traced to an even earlier time among the various tribes of the Algonquin people who traveled on and fished these waters. Our location on the Atlantic Ocean and surrounding the great waters and islands of Narragansett Bay has helped to create a boatbuilding, commercial fishing, and recreational boating culture that endures to this day. Some of the state's earliest shipyards are now gone, but several survive to repair, replace, and rebuild today's modern fleet of draggers, lobster boats, ferries, yachts, and work boats.

In Newport and elsewhere on the East Bay, there is a surprising rebirth and renewed interest in shipbuilding and other maritime skills. In addition to numerous small and medium size ship fitters and small boat builders, the **International Yacht Restoration School** (Newport/Bristol) is busy preparing the next generation of highly skilled boat builders, restorers, and marine mechanics. (www.iyrs.org)

Why
Rhode Island
Matters!

Educator to the World

Each year people come to Rhode Island from more than 100 countries to attend our world-class colleges and universities. From the University of Rhode Island to Johnson & Wales University, Rhode Island College, Brown University, Providence College, Rhode Island School of Design, Salve Regina University, Bryant University, Block Island University, New England Institute of Technology, and the Community College of Rhode Island, tens of thousands of students are stimulated, inspired, educated, and sent out to improve the world. Here they make lifelong friends, form partnerships, marry and start families, and build new businesses that create jobs and make a difference.

Our quality schools of higher education are a huge magnet that attracts the best and brightest to our state. When students and their parents arrive here they are amazed by so much they we often overlook: the architecture, the natural beauty of the landscape, and the beaches. That is why many students become permanent residents after graduation.

They find what those of us who love this state have found:

Rhode Island is a great place to call *home*.

Why
Rhode Island
Matters!

Treasure: Roger Williams Park & Zoo

Roger Williams Park & Zoo is like taking a trip back in time. The layout of the park is evocative of an earlier time, with its 19th century design by Horace W.S. Cleveland who borrowed many ideas from the genius behind New York's Central Park and Boston Commons, Frederick Law Olmsted. The park has won awards and its land and building protected in perpetuity with its placement on the National Register of Historic Places. (See more at www.rwpzoo.org)

The Roger Williams Park Zoo is the nation's third oldest, part of Roger Williams Park, and features numerous exhibits, including Plains of Africa, the African Pavilion, Madagascar, Marco Polo Trail, and Tropical America. The land for the park, some 430 acres, was donated to the City of Providence by Betsey Williams (great-great-granddaughter of Roger Williams) upon her death in 1871.

The zoo is surrounded by the park's botanical garden, natural history museum, butterfly garden, Carousel Village, Benedict Temple to Music, a Japanese Garden, walking trails, ten lakes, and numerous water features. Near the Elmwood Avenue entrance to the park is the majestic Roger Williams Casino (1896), not a gambling house, but a colonial revival two story mansion with a large ballroom that is a favorite venue for weddings, fundraisers, and dinners.

Why Rhode Island Matters!

America's First Resort

Rhode Island was America's first tourist destination even before there was an America.

Early explorer (and first tourist), **Giovanni da Verrazano**, toured around Block Island in 1524. He thought it looked somewhat like the Greek island of Rhodes, thus the misnomer later explorers placed on Aquidneck Island and the subsequent moniker of "Rhode Island". Verrazano also explored some of the 38 islands of Narragansett Bay. Born in Tuscany, Italy, and a well-known pirate whose previous career was devoted to capturing gold laden ships headed for Spain, he sailed for North America under the sponsorship of King Francis I of France. With two ships, he explored the east coast from Nova Scotia to North Carolina, including New York Bay, in search of a shorter route to China.

While the first hotels and clam shacks were yet to be built in the Ocean State, Verrazano apparently liked what he saw and went home to tell others about our ample shore and pristine waters. He later made two more voyages to North America. Other explorers would follow.

Each year millions of visitors come to Rhode Island, some retracing the voyage of the First Tourist.

Why Rhode Island Matters!

Natural Wonders

Carved from the leavings of a vast glacier over 10,000 years ago, Rhode Island is blessed with amazing natural wonders and water resources that have provided sustenance, habitat and recreation for generations of fish, fowl, and humans beings.

Narragansett Bay

Narragansett Bay is our state's greatest natural wonder, nearly 150 square miles in size, dividing the state into two parts, east and west, and reaching into southern parts of Massachusetts. The bay forms the region's largest estuary and is the recipient of the water of three rivers---the Sakonnet, Providence, and Taunton.

Some 38 islands are scattered throughout the bay, with the three largest being Aquidneck Island (Newport), Conanicus Island (Jamestown), and Prudence Island. The bay opens to the Atlantic Ocean about 25 miles south of Providence.

The bay is home to more than 60 species of fish and shell-fish, including flounder, mussels, lobster, oysters, quahogs, tautog, mackerel, striped bass, sea snails, and crabs. It is also home to fishermen, boaters, and commercial vessel traffic.

Why Rhode Island Matters!

Natural Wonders

Beaches

Rhode Island is blessed with many natural resources: farm land, forests, lakes, rivers, swamps, fish, deer, and other wildlife. The most popular are the state's 100+ beaches.

The best beach?

It depends who you ask. At the top of any Rhode Islander's list is **Narragansett Town Beach**. This flat white-sand beach hugs the shore of Narragansett Bay for a mile just north of Block Island Sound and the Atlantic Ocean. The beach is in the shadow of the famed Towers, a 19th century stone structure straddling Ocean Road that was once part of a much larger casino that burned to the ground.

Other favorite beaches are:

Easton Beach (aka First Beach), Newport

Scarborough State Beach, Narragansett

Roger Wheeler Memorial Beach (aka Sand Hill Cove), Narragansett

Misquamicut State Beach, Westerly

Why
Rhode Island
Matters!

Block Island

It was called **Manisses** by the Narragansett Indians but named Block Island by Dutch explorer **Adriaen Block** after his visit there in 1614. Officially incorporated in 1672 as New Shoreham, the island is a thriving tourist destination and home for 900 year-round residents that has preserved much of its natural state and provides a wonderful escape from a busy world. Just ten miles off the southern coast of Rhode Island, it has been called "one of the last great places in the Western Hemisphere" by the Nature Conservancy. *It is one of my favorite places in the world!*

Block Island is blessed with at least 8 beaches and 365 fresh water ponds. It is a key stopover for birds flying south for the winter and each autumn birders from around the world come to observe the many species of birds. There's a wide variety of fish around the ten square mile island and a quahog fishery in the Great Salt Pond. Two lighthouses help keep sailors safe from its rocky shores.

Hotels, B&Bs, inns, restaurants, and peace await the visitor. Access is by car ferry or high-speed ferry from New London (CT), Galilee and Newport (RI), and Montauk (Long Island, NY). Or you can fly into Block Island Airport from Westerly, Warwick, Groton (CT), and other sites. More information: www.blockisland.com

Why Rhode Island Matters!

Man-Made Wonders

Newport Mansions

The *City by the Sea* boasts an amazing collection of Gilded Age mansions that were once the summer homes, or "cottages," of New York's wealthiest families. Today, more than a dozen homes are open for tours and will take you back to another time. *Visit!*

Providence Architecture

Providence was built on seven hills (only six remain) and dates back to the arrival of Roger Williams here in 1636. Providence features the best preserved and largest colonial architecture of any city in the United States. For an amazing look at the buildings and history of this great city, see **PPS/AIAri Guide to Providence Architecture,** by William McKenzie Woodward.

Claiborne Pell Bridge (Newport Bridge)

This suspension bridge, built in 3-1/2 years, opened on June 28, 1969. The bridge overall is 2.13 miles long and connects Conanicut Island (Jamestown) and Aquidneck Island (Newport). It carries a 4-lane highway (Rt. 138) rising 215 feet above the East Passage of Narragansett Bay. Built at a cost of $54,742,000 ($320 million in 2009 dollars), it averages 27,000 vehicles per day.

Why
Rhode Island
Matters!

Man-Made Wonders

Cliff Walk, Newport

This 3.5 mile walkway overlooks the ocean running parallel to Bellevue Avenue beginning at Memorial Boulevard and ending at the corner of Bellevue and Coggeshall Avenues. The walkway has existed, in one form or another, since the 1850's. One notable feature is the **40 Steps** running down to the water at the end of Narragansett Avenue. It was a gathering place for servants and workers from the mansions in the late 1800's and early 1900's.

Rhode Island State House

The seat of power for the state is in the halls and chambers of the Rhode Island State House. It's that huge white Georgia marble building on Smith Hill, overlooking the city of Providence, built between 1895 and 1904. Designed in the late 1890's by McKim, Mead and White, it features the world's fourth largest unsupported marble dome (after the third place Taj Mahal) and a 14-foot tall, 500-pound bronze statue of "The Independent Man." The statue, covered in gold leaf, was cast by Gorham Manufacturing Company in Providence using bronze recycled from the statue of liberator Simon Bolivar that had stood in Central Park. Costing $3,000, it was placed atop the State House dome on December 18, 1899. The General Assembly first met in the State House on January 1, 1901.

Birthplace of Greatness

Big things
can definitely begin
in a small place.

Rhode Island
has been the
launching pad for
many nation-shaking,
world changing people
and their
great ideas.

Why Rhode Island Matters!

Entrepreneurial Families

There is a long history of family businesses in Rhode Island from painter Gilbert Stuart's family in North Kingstown with the construction and operation of the first water-powdered snuff mill in the Americas in the 1700's to the multi-generational Schartner farming and retail fruit and vegetable business in North Kingstown.

Rhode Island is also home to the oldest continuously operated family owned business in the United States, **Ashaway Line & Twine Manufacturing Company**, founded in 1824 by Captain Lester Crandall. The company is located in the village of Ashaway in the town of Hopkinton. Crandall invented and perfected several line making machines. The firm, six generations old and still owned by the Crandall family, originally produced fishing line, but is now a leading maker of strings for racket sports, braided twines for the textile industry, and suture thread used in operating rooms worldwide. The company has always innovated. It produced the first commercial nylon product (fishing line) in the world when DuPont looked for a use for their new filament product in 1939. Ashaway also used Dacron the first year it was introduced by DuPont (1952) and in 1977 introduced the first Kevlar tennis string. In 2009, Ashaway perfected their ZyWeave™ core technology and introduced ZyMax62 badminton string to the sports world, the thinnest string ever produced for rackets.

Leaders never look backward, always forward!

Why
Rhode Island
Matters!

Visionary Entrepreneurs

This state has always been a hotbed for entrepreneurs.
Whether the idea is their original concept or they run with someone else's idea and make it into something bigger, better, and more dynamic, Rhode Islanders know how to make things happen---creating jobs, creating businesses, and creating wealth. Here are the brief stories of some amazing visionary entrepreneurs.

GTECH (Guy Snowden & Victor Markowicz, 1980)

This company, begun as Gaming Dimensions in Providence, became the world's largest lottery services company before being purchased by Italian lottery company Lottomatica Group in 2006. GTECH is now a 2.9 billion Euros (2011) firm, headquartered in Rome, Italy. GTECH still maintains manufacturing facilities and offices in Rhode Island.

Textron (Textile mill owner Royal Little, 1923)

Originally founded as a small yarn company in 1923, Royal Little decided in 1952 to combine dissimilar businesses to create the first modern conglomerate. Though Little claimed to have lost more than $100,000,000 over his career, his perseverance was winning. The company, based in downtown Providence, has sales of $10.5 billion (2009) and consists of several divisions including Bell Helicopter, Cessna Aircraft, E-Z-GO golf carts, and others.

25

Why Rhode Island Matters!

Visionary Entrepreneurs

Hemenway's, Capital Grille, Bugaboo Creek Steak House (Restaurant Creator Edward Phelps "Ned" Grace III)

His first restaurant in Rhode Island, Hemenway's Restaurant in downtown Providence, was immediately deemed the best seafood restaurant in the state. He named it in honor of his entrepreneurial grandfather, Charles Martin Hemenway. His next two concepts, Capital Grille and Bugaboo Creek Steak House, also launched here; both grew. He added several additional units of each concept. The company went public in 1994. Capital Grille is now owned by Darden Restaurants (Olive Garden, Red Lobster). Grace continues life as a serial entrepreneur based in Florida.

HASBRO (Brothers Henry and Helal Hassenfeld, 1923)

An entire history of toys began in the Ocean State with the 1923 creation of a textile remnant company called Hassenfeld Brothers that later became Hasbro (1968). Initially, the company made pencil boxes, doctor and nurse kits, and other small items. The purchase of rights to Mr. Potato Head in 1952 marked a national success in the toy business. This was followed by G.I. Joe in 1964 and other successful toys followed. The company now owns more than a dozen brands, is a leader in character licensing for film and cartoon media, and becoming involved in new films based on its brands. Sales in 2011 topped $4.29 billion.

Why Rhode Island Matters!

Visionary Entrepreneurs

FM Global (Mill owner Zachariah Allen, 1835)

In 1835, textile mill owner **Zachariah Allen** requested a reduction in his insurance premiums after making substantial improvements to his building to mitigate damage in the event of fire. As the concept of loss prevention and control was unheard of at that time, his request was denied. Allen grouped a number of like-minded mill owners together and formed the Manufacturers Mutual Fire Insurance Company. Premiums were reduced for all members and at year-end all remaining premiums were returned to the policyholders as dividends. The company continued expanding and adding additional geographic areas, beginning in Boston. The present FM Global is a combination of three mutual insurance companies that merged in 1999. The firm is now a $5.1 billion enterprise with clients in 120 countries.

Baking Powder Invented & First Produced Here (Rumford Chemical Works, East Providence, 1869)

Eben Norton Horsford began the manufacture of chemicals in 1867. Two years later, the business became Rumford Chemical Works. Horsford formulated and patented Rumford Baking Powder, the first calcium phosphate baking powder. Soon after, the firm became one of largest and most successful chemical plants in the country. Rumford Baking Powder is still a national brand.

Why Rhode Island Matters!

Women Who Matter

Women have always played a major role in the development of Rhode Island. You should know that these women are a big reason **Why Rhode Island Matters!**

Anne Hutchinson was the first and only woman founder of a town in colonial times, establishing the town of Portsmouth on Aquidneck Island in 1638 when she was 47. She had previously borne 14 children, undergone excommunication from Massachusetts Bay Colony for her Puritan beliefs and public preaching, and battled early settler William Coddington, who then went farther south to found Newport.

Gertrude Johnson and **Mary Wales** opened a small business education school in downtown Providence in 1914. They taught typing, shorthand, and bookkeeping. After WWII, two war veterans, **Morris Gaebe** and **Edward Triangolo**, with their wives, purchased the successful school so that Miss Johnson and Miss Wales could retire. They honored the women founders by keeping their names on the business as it evolved over the next 50 years to become the internationally-known Johnson & Wales University with four campuses around the U.S.

Why
Rhode Island
Matters!

Women Who Matter

Here are a few more Rhode Island women who matter.

Helen Adelia Rowe Metcalf, a member of the Centennial Women who had raised funds to mount a Rhode Island exhibit at the 1876 Centennial Exposition, persuaded the group to donate $1,675 left over after the exposition to start what became the **Rhode Island School of Design (RISD)** in 1877. Metcalf ran the school until 1895, succeeded by her daughter, **Eliza Greene Metcalf Radeke** who directed the school until 1931. RISD is the nation's leading private art school. The start of Fall, 2012 classes marks the school's 135th year.

Anna Coffey Haven (aka Anne Philomena Haven) has been credited with using the proceeds of her late husband's life insurance policy to purchase a horse-drawn lunch cart in 1893 that became **Haven Brothers Diner**, famous for its hotdogs, and continues to operate from a silver trailer next to city hall in Providence. Her family helped the fledgling start-up. At the time, her brother-in-law **Frank Haven** was the city's sergeant-at-arms and managed the dining room in nearby Union Station. The business name likely was derived from this family involvement in the early years.

Haven Brothers Diner is open daily from 5pm till 3am. Go in and order, "One, all the way." *You'll enjoy a delicious hotdog!*

Leading
With the
Best!

Rhode Island
Matters!

Why
Rhode Island
Matters!

World's Best Made Here

Looff Carousel

The greatest carver and builder of wooden carousels, Danish master woodcarver Charles I.D. Looff, made his home in Riverside (East Providence) in the 1890's. Looff was known for his beautiful carousels with exquisitely hand-carved animals. His first project, after years as a New York City furniture builder, was his hand-made carousel (1876) for the amusement park at Coney Island (NY).

Crescent Park, later called "the Coney Island of the East," had recently opened in Rhode Island (1886) and the park's owner wanted the best carousel available for his venue. He contracted with Looff, to build the largest carousel ever. Looff, having lost his property to eminent domain in the city of New York, decided to move to Rhode Island. He later showcased an even nicer carousel to customers and built a workshop next door to work on his special brand of "merry-go-rounds."

Kids of all ages can still take a ride on the Charles I.D. Looff Carousel at Crescent Park on Bullocks Point Avenue in the Riverside section of East Providence. Another Looff Carousel, built in 1895, can be found in Slater Park in Pawtucket. Both operate from May/June through September/October.

Why
Rhode Island
Matters!

Oldest 4th of July Parade

The first is also the best. Big, too!

The Bristol 4th of July Parade is the first, oldest and longest continuously run Independence Day parade in the United States. First organized and run by residents of this quaint and fervently patriotic town on the East side of Narragansett Bay on July 4th, 1785, the parade has persevered into its fourth century of celebrating the founding of our nation. 2012 marks the 227th year for this annual parade.

Plan to attend and be part of next year's parade? There's a whole week of activities, including concerts, contests and plenty of food. A fireworks show lights up the night before the big parade, with beautiful rockets and displays rising up over the waters of the Bay. The parade kicks off the next morning from Chestnut Street and Hope Street (Rt. 114) at 10:30am and ends at High Street between State Street and Bradford Street.

Get there early. Most spots along the main route are reserved by 5am by locals and parade fanatics in the know. Lawn chairs and assorted other props seem to mark every square foot of lawn and sidewalk. For those who can't be there, the parade is annually broadcast live on ABC6 and streams live on the internet. (See: www.July4thBristolRI.com)

Why
Rhode Island
Matters!

We Nurture Great Artists

We have been the home to great artists dating from the native Algonquins who created wampum from quahog shells for use in trade. This history of great artists has continued and includes the architects, engineers, and designers of buildings, ships, and machinery that have driven commerce and industry here for more than 300 years. The field has been encouraged by the establishment (1877) of the Rhode Island School of Design (RISD), ranked consistently as the nation's number one private art and design college. Through the visionary work of both artists and supportive educators like RISD, Rhode Islanders have played a key role in advancing the field of art and design worldwide.

Leading Painters

Gilbert Stuart

Saunderstown, Rhode Island was the 1755 birthplace of **Gilbert Stuart**, portrait artist of the most famous painting of President George Washington that is featured in the Capitol Building in Washington, DC, the Rhode Island State House, and on the U.S. one dollar bill. It is believed to be the most widely circulated portrait in history. Wherever the dollar is, part of Rhode Island and Rhode Island's history is there as well. Stuart's birthplace is now open to the public and includes his home, two working water wheels, several exhibits, and guided tours. (www.gilbertstuartmuseum.com)

Why
Rhode Island
Matters!

We Nurture Great Artists

John La Farge

Painter and stained glass artist, **John La Farge**, who lived in Newport in the 1850's, befriended French sculptor **Auguste Bartholdi** during his first visit to the United States. Bartholdi met his future wife here and in 1871 the marriage took place at the La Farge home. La Farge's home was also where Bartholdi met architect Richard Morris Hunt. A few years later, Bartholdi would design and build a statue named *Liberty Enlightening the World*. We know it as the Statue of Liberty. Hunt would design and oversee the construction of the 154-foot high stone pedestal for the statue on Bedloe's Island (now Liberty Island). La Farge's art can be seen in the grand murals inside Boston's Trinity Church and in elegant stained glass evident in numerous residential homes.

Leading Painters of More Recent Vintage

Leading the list are **Anthony Tomaselli** and **Joe Szarek**. Tomaselli, an inspiring teacher and prolific painter of unique New England scenes---Providence, Block Island, Maine---is based in Rhode Island. (See: www.anthonytomaselli.com) Szarek is a gifted impressionist-style painter of landscapes, seascapes, still life, and a series of icebergs captured during a trip to Newfoundland. Sza- rek, formerly of North Kingstown and a RISD graduate, is now based in New Mexico. His work can be seen locally at the New- port Art Museum, Newport, RI. (See: www.joeszarek.com)

Why
Rhode Island
Matters!

We Promote Great Music Here

Rhode Island loves, supports and promotes great music in every genre. There is a long list of successful musical artists and promoters who have made this a haven (some would say "heaven") for music. They include former RISD student and rocker **David Byrne** (Talking Heads), composer **Bill Conti** (Theme from "Rocky"), composer and showman **George M. Cohan*** ("I'm a Yankee Doodle Dandy," "You're a Grand Old Flag," and "Over There"), **George Wein**, who created and still produces the long-running Newport Jazz Festival (and many others), and **Donald King**, who produced the Providence Sound Session, and now runs Fete, a music venue in the Olneyville neighborhood.

This state also is home to more than a hundred clubs and live venues where music of every fashion is showcased, danced to, and enjoyed. New musical voices here include **The Hummingbird Trio**, three young women with Andrews Sisters-style harmonies and a repertoire of American standards. Rhode Island is a great place to create, to play, to find one's voice, to find fellow players, and to establish and base an exciting and productive life in the musical arts.

**Not so incidentally, Rhode Island native George M. Cohan is the only Broadway person to have his statue in Times Square where it looks out over the lights and theaters of "The Great White Way."*

Why
Rhode Island
Matters!

We Nurture Great Writers Here

We encourage, nurture, and sustain great writers here. Many are of local renown; some of national and even international acclaim. In every field of writing, there are great talents who got their start here and many more who are creating future classics even as you read these words(!).

We have homegrown writers and others who find our state a great place to create. They include former Brown University professor and playwright **Paula Vogel** ("How I Learned to Drive"), Rhode Island historians **Dr. Patrick T. Conley, Tim Cranston,** and **Scott Malloy,** novelists **Ann Hood** (The Knitting Circle, The Red Thread), **Jhumpa Lahir** (Unaccustomed Earth, The Namesake), and **Betty Cotter** (Roberta's Woods), fantasy and horror writer **H.P. Lovecraft**, and children's author/illustrator **Chris Van Allsberg** (Polar Express).

If you are a writer or want to be a writer, Rhode Island is a perfect place to be inspired, to sort out your thoughts, to be refreshed, and to craft your story.

Why
Rhode Island
Matters!

Leader in Military Matters (Then & Now)

Our state has been a leader in military matters from the very beginning and has developed solutions to address many challenges, particularly during wartime.

The first formal, government authorized navy in the colonies and the Western Hemisphere was established by the Rhode Island General Assembly on June 12, 1775. Shortly afterward, George Washington began acquiring ships and commissioned the schooner *Hannah* on September 5, 1775. The official date of the establishment of the U.S. Navy was October 13, 1775.

The first **Naval War College** was established on October 6, 1884 in Newport on Coaster's Harbor Island in a building that previously had been the Newport Asylum for the Poor. Until the establishment of the college, all classes were conducted aboard navy ships.

The **U.S. Naval Torpedo Station** was founded on Goat Island in Newport in 1869. Newport was the largest producer of torpedoes in WWI and WWII. In 1951, it became the Underwater Weapons Research and Engineering Station. In 1992, the command was reorganized as the Naval Undersea Warfare Center.

Why
Rhode Island
Matters!

Leader in Military Matters (Then & Now)

U.S. Navy Seabees

The Seabees, a battalion of Navy construction engineers founded (January 1942), at Quonset Point Naval Air Station (North Kingstown) at the beginning of World War II, built airfields all over the world, and popularized the often-imitated Quonset Hut (1941) that was flown in as a kit and assembled on military bases wherever U.S. armed forces were assigned worldwide. More than 325,000 men served with the Seabees in World War II, fighting and building in more than 400 locations before the war's end.

The motto of the Seabees is *Construmus Batumius*, or *We Build, We Fight*. A logo, the Fighting Bee, was created by Rhode Islander Frank J. Iafrate. Iafrate also built the Seabee statue that now stands guard at the site of the Seabee Museum at Davisville.

The Seabee Museum and Memorial Park is located at the entrance to Quonset Point/Davisville Industrial Park. It is open daily from 10am-2pm. Visit! (See: www.seabeesmuseum.com)

First
and
Unique!

Rhode Island
Matters!

Why
Rhode Island
Matters!

Sports Matter Here

Babe Ruth played here first.

Before he was a winning pitcher for the Boston Red Sox, and prior to his sale in 1919 to the New York Yankees (where he switched to playing right field), Babe Ruth lived on the Southside of Providence. He played one year for the Providence Grays (1914) at the long gone Messer Field in the Olneyville neighborhood. At the time, the Grays were a minor league team, part of the Eastern League. After leaving the Yankees, Ruth occasionally pitched exhibition games with the Boston Braves (circa 1935) at historic Cardines Field in Newport.

Today Cardines Field is home to the Newport Gulls, a team of college baseball players recruited from around the Northeast. They offer an exciting summer schedule of baseball in a congenial family atmosphere across the street from Newport Harbor (America's Cup Avenue & West Marlborough Street, Newport; 401-847-1398).

Messer Field may be gone, but the Grays are back. The Providence Grays Vintage Base Ball Club, founded in 1998 by baseball aficionado Tim Norton, has revived the playing of vintage 19th century baseball with the development of competitive teams (now more than 200 around the U.S.) and a regular schedule of exhibition games at venues around New England. The team is based in East Providence (401-787-6276).

Why
Rhode Island
Matters!

Sports Matter Here

Longest Baseball Game in History!

Rhode Island is a great place to make sports history.

The longest game in baseball history was played between the Rochester Red Wings and the Pawtucket Red Sox at McCoy Stadium in 1981. The game began on Saturday, April 18, 1981 and finally was called at 4:07am on Easter Sunday morning. It was the end of the 32nd inning and a total of 19 fans remained. Among the soon-to-be-famous players on the field were Cal Ripkin, Jr. for Rochester and Wade Boggs for the PawSox.

The game was resumed at the next meeting of the two teams on June 23, 1981. The PawSox won the game in the bottom of the 33rd inning. The Red Wings had 18 hits to the PawSox 21 hits. The final score was 3-2.

Total time for the game was 8 hours, 25 minutes.

The Pawtucket Red Sox is the Triple-A affiliate of the Boston Red Sox and is based at McCoy Stadium, one of the most modern and beautiful stadiums anywhere. *Go see a game!*

Why
Rhode Island
Matters!

A Perfect Place for FIRSTS!

Pulitzer Prizes

The first Pulitzer Prize for journalism ever given to an *entire staff* of a newspaper was awarded to the reporters and photographers of the *Providence Journal Bulletin* in 1953 for their coverage of a story a bank hold-up on September 30, 1952. The annual Pulitzer Prizes, envisioned by publisher Joseph Pulitzer (1904) and administered by the Columbia School of Journalism (NY), recognizes excellence in journalism. The *Providence Journal*, over more than 190 years of newspaper publishing, has won four Pulitzer Prizes.

First Act of Violence Against British Authority

Rhode Islanders committed the first act of violence against Britain's authority in America by destroying the British sloop *Liberty* on July 19, 1769 in Newport. This act preceded by nearly three years the more famous burning of the British schooner *Gaspee* in Narragansett Bay on June 9, 1772.

First in Automation

The world's first fully–mechanized post office, called *Project Turn-key*, was opened in Providence on October 20, 1960. The huge one-story automated U.S. Post Office facility cost $20,000,000 ($145,000,000 in 2009 dollars).

Why Rhode Island Matters!

A Perfect Place for FIRSTS!

First Polo Matches

The first polo matches in the United States were conducted in Newport in 1877. The matches became a staple of the short summer seasons in the 1880's during Newport's storied gilded age. Polo has been a regular feature on Aquidneck Island ever since. Today, polo matches are held at the Newport Polo Club at Glen farm in Portsmouth (Rt. 138), June through September. Details are at: www.newportinternationalpolo.com.

The First "Factor"

We may have the most interesting weather anywhere. So it's no surprise we've had our own way of talking about it.

Long before author and television host Bill O'Reilly created his hit cable show, "The O'Reilly Factor," Rhode Island and Southeastern New England residents had the already well-known **Ghiorse Factor**. The Ghiorse Factor was not a TV show, but rather a number to indicate what the weather was expected to be and how nice it was for working outdoors. It was developed by meteorologist John Ghiorse in the 1970's while he was at NBC-10 (WJAR). A Ghiorse Factor of "10" was the best. A Ghiorse Factor of "1" or "2" was a projection of "not-so-nice outside."

Why Rhode Island Matters!

A Perfect Place for FIRSTS!

Oldest Philanthropist Trust in the U.S.

On his death bed, Rhode Island co-founder Dr. John Clarke (1609-1676), included in his will the establishment of a trust for charitable purposes. Today the John Clarke Trust is the oldest and longest operating trust in the nation, with a mission to support "the relief of the poor or bringing up of children unto learning," and is focused on support for non-profits serving residents on Aquidneck Island. The trust is administered by Bank of America in Boston.

The Arcade - First Enclosed Mall

Despite numerous claims by malls and shopping centers around the country, the 3-story Arcade, situated on property sandwiched between Westminster Street on the west and Weybosset Street on the east in downtown Providence, is the oldest enclosed mall structure still in existence. It was built over two years, 1827-28, in a Greek revival style. Architects J.C. Bucklin and Russell Warren designed the building with 12-ton columns that are still the largest monoliths in America with the exception of those in the cathedral of St. John the Divine in New York City. Bear Rock Ledge in nearby Johnston was the source of the granite pillars. Preceding the arrival of trains and trucks, they were hauled to the downtown site one at a time by 15 yoke of oxen.

Why
Rhode Island
Matters!

First in Religious Freedom

First Baptist Church, Providence

The First Baptist Church in America was formed in Providence in 1638 by Roger Williams. Williams had been holding services at his home for a year before the official founding of the church. The First Baptist Meetinghouse (on South Main Street) was built in 1774-75 and was affiliated for many years with Brown University.

First Jewish Synagogue, Newport

Touro Synagogue, oldest synagogue in North America, was designed by Peter Harrison, and built in Newport (1759-1763). The building (85 Touro Street) was dedicated on December 2, 1763 and faces east toward Jerusalem. Newport's original Jeshuat Israel congregation established the synagogue in 1658 when 15 Spanish and Portuguese Jewish families arrived from the West Indies. Today's congregation follows an orthodox tradition. The synagogue was listed on the National Register of Historic Places in 1966.

Old Narragansett Church, Wickford

This Episcopal Church was built in 1707. Portrait artist Gilbert Stuart was baptized in the church in 1756. The building was listed on the National Register of Historic Places in 1973.

Why
Rhode Island
Matters!

First in Industry

Samuel Slater (1768-1835)

Samuel Slater, following an apprenticeship in the Arkwright wa-ter-powered textile mills in England, arrived in the U.S. (1789) to apply his knowledge to the cotton-spinning businesses on the East Coast. He joined with Quaker **Moses Brown** to build his first mill (Slater Mill) in Pawtucket in 1793. Slater's management talent later led him to create a mill town, **Slatersville**, now part of North Smithfield. Thus began the **Industrial Revolution** that led the nation's rise to great economic power. Slater was also called the "Father of the American Sunday School System," establishing Bible classes in his mills to teach employees reading and writing.

George H. Corliss (1817-1888)

George H. Corliss was a mechanical engineer and inventor who developed labor-saving devices and a steam engine in 1848 that soon was recognized as the most efficient. His Providence-based company, Corliss Steam Engine, became the largest producer of steam engines in the U.S. Corliss went on to hold 60 patents that helped save time and manpower in factories and businesses. A special Corliss Engine, driving a one mile long shaft, powered nearly all of the exhibits at the 1876 Philadelphia Centennial Ex-position. *Rhode Island is a GREAT place to innovate!*

Why Rhode Island Matters!

More FIRSTS!

Rhode Island was home to the first open **golf tournament** in 1895.

The first **circus** in the country was hosted in Newport in 1774.

The first street in the U.S. to use **gas illuminated street lights** was Pelham Street in Newport.

The first **law against slavery** in North America was enacted by Rhode Island on May 18, 1652.

The first **American bred horse** of the Colonial era was the Narragansett Pacer.

The first **torpedo boat**, *Stiletto*, was built in Bristol, RI in 1887.

The first national **lawn tennis** championships were hosted in Rhode Island in 1899.

The first **auto race** in the U.S. was held in Newport in 1895.

The first discount department store in the U.S., **Ann and Hope**, was opened in Rhode Island in 1953.

Bradley Hospital in East Providence was the first **psychiatric hospital for children** (1931) in the United States.

Why
Rhode Island
Matters!

Our Unique Foods

One thing Rhode Islanders agree on is that we like to eat. We have our own unique food items with our own names. These are foods to be embraced, celebrated, and most of all---eaten!

We've got **grinders** (sub sandwiches or hoagies), **coffee milk** (coffee syrup mixed with milk), **stuffies** (clam meat and bread baked in a quahog [clam] shell and served hot with lemon), **hot wieners** (short thin hotdogs with a "secret" ground beef sauce, chopped onions and celery salt served on a steamed bun), **cabinets** (milk shakes), **clamcakes** (crisp deep fried "sinkers" made from flour, clam juice, chopped clams, and pepper), **chowder** (clear or white clam chowder---never red), **jonnycakes** (pancake-like cakes made from white flint-ground cornmeal, salt, sugar, water), and **Del's Lemonade** (lemon-flavored Italian ice), and more.

Official State Foods

The **quahog** is the official state shellfish. **Striped bass** is the official state fish. The state fruit is the **Rhode Island Greening Apple**. The state bird is the always deliciously edible **Rhode Island Red** (chicken). **Coffee milk** was named the official state drink in 1993, edging out perennial summer favorite, Del's Lemonade.

If a people is known by its food, then Rhode Islanders must be known as creative, innovative, and yes---unique!

51

Why
Rhode Island
Matters!

Our Unique Foods

Mayor's Own Marinara Sauce

Developed from his Mother's recipe, former Providence Mayor **Vincent A. "Buddy" Cianci** began selling his locally bottled sauce in 1994 with all proceeds funding $1,000 college scholarships for students graduating from Providence high schools. More than 100 scholarships have been awarded. Though he has been out of office for many years, but now heard daily on *The Buddy Cianci Show* (WPRO/WEAN), the sauce continues selling locally and across the country to support his scholarship program.

Coffee Syrup

Rhode Islander's love their coffee and anything made with coffee in it. Coffee milk, coffee ice cream, and coffee beans covered with chocolate. Fortunately, there is a local connection.

Autocrat Coffee, the world's leading producer of coffee syrup extract with ownership of both the Autocrat and Eclipse brands, is a fourth-generation Rhode Island coffee roaster and extract manufacturer based in Lincoln, RI. They're number one.

Coffee lovers everywhere can get all the coffee-based products they need from Autocrat.

Why
Rhode Island
Matters!

A Perfect Menu of Rhode Island Classic Cuisine

Breakfast
+Rhody Fresh Milk   +Allie's Donuts
+Johnnycakes with Maple syrup & applesauce

Lunch
+Rhode Island Quahog Chowder (Clear Broth)
+Grinder (Italian cold cuts with olive oil and red vinegar)
+Quahog Chili (at Duffy's Tavern in NK)

Dinner
+Native Lobster
+Fish & Chips
+Steamed Littlenecks (Quahogs)
+Steamed Mussels in white wine

Snacks, Late Night & Anytime
+Del's Lemonade
+Hot Wieners, Fries, Coffee Milk
+Dough Boys
+Yacht Club Soda
+Cabinet (milkshake)
+Dynamites (Sloppy Joe-style sandwich served on a grinder roll)
+Stuffies (baked stuffed quahogs)
+Chowder & Clam Cakes
+Hotdog all the way (at Haven Brothers)

Why Rhode Island Matters!

Rhode Island Red Hen: State Bird
It's What's For Breakfast [and Dinner!]

The Rhode Island Red Hen is a delicious Ocean State native that is also the official state bird.

It is America's best known breed of fowl, a combination of several breeds, and probably the best known breed in the world. Hens weigh around six pounds and roosters can weigh over eight pounds. It's a good layer of brown eggs, laying 250-300 per year, and also makes a great roasting chicken. The Rhode Island Red chicken was originally developed in the 1850's by a farmer in Adamsville, a small village in the town of Little Compton. It has been the leading chicken in the commercial poultry industry ever since.

Some other facts about Rhode Island Reds:

Rhode Island Reds also make good show birds and are entered in state and local farm fairs nationwide.

In 1925, a commemorative sculpture by Henry L. Norton was erected in Adamsville to recognize the importance of this hearty breed.

Why Rhode Island Matters!

Your Ideas Welcome

Rhode Island's history is long and our accomplishments are many. There are certainly many more stories, more facts, and more reasons why Rhode Island matters. Send me your favorites and I'll include them in the next volume of this book. If I include your contribution, I will send you a signed copy of the next edition of **Why Rhode Island Matters!** ™

Write me care of:
Shoreline Press
P.O. Box 110
Slocum, RI 02877

Email me:
annmariemarshall8@hotmail.com

Interested in moving to Rhode Island? Contact me!
Military Veterans: I am a VA Specialist
Contatc me at: 401-269-9827

Here's wishing you a most successful year!

Why
Rhode Island
Matters!

LINKS & WEB SITES
FOR MORE INFORMATION

Ashaway Line & Twine Manufacturing Company
www.ashawayusa.com

Bristol 4th of July Parade
www.July4thBristolRI.com

GTECH
www.gtech.com

HASBRO
www.hasbro.com

HELIN Library Consortium
www.helin.uri.edu

Hemenway's
www.hemenwaysrestaurant.com

John Clarke Trust
www.johnclarkesociety.org

Newport Gulls
www.newportgulls.com

Why
Rhode Island
Matters!

LINKS & WEB SITES

Ocean State Libraries
www.oslri.org

Providence Athenaeum
www.providenceathenaeum.org

Providence Grays
www.providencegrays.org

Providence Journal
www.projo.com

Redwood Library and Athenaeum
www.redwood1747.org

Rhody Fresh Milk
www.rhodyfresh.com

Textron
www.textron.com

Yacht Club Soda
www.yachtclubsoda.com

Why
Rhode Island
Matters!

Bibliography

Want to learn more about my wonderful Rhode Island?

Here are a few of the many books and other resources you can consult to guide you into our history, features, and people.

Beaulieu, Linda. *The Providence and Rhode Island Cookbook*. Insiders' Guide, 2006.

Bodah, Paula M. *Rhode Island: The Spirit of America*. Harry N. Abrams, Inc., 2000.

Brown, Seth. *Rhode Island Curiosities*. Insiders' Guide, 2007.

Collins, Andrew. *Moon Handbooks Rhode Island*. Avalon Travel Publishing, 2003.

Conley, Patrick T. *Rhode Island's Founders: From Settlement to Statehood*. The History Press, 2010.

Henderson, Linda L., Editor. *Rhode Island Almanac*. The Providence Journal Company, 1992.

Lehnnert, Tim. *Rhode Island 101*. MacIntyre Purcell Publishing Inc., 2009.

Why
Rhode Island
Matters!

Bibliography

McLoughlin, William G. *Rhode Island: A History*. W.W. Norton & Company, 1978.

Rogers, Barbara Radcliffe and Rogers, Juliette. *Secret Providence and Newport*. ECW Press, 2002.

Newport Cliff Walk
www.cliffwalk.com

Newport Mansions
www.newportmansions.org

Official State Web Site
www.state.ri.us

Rhode Island Info & Stories
www.quahog.org

RILINK
www.ricat.net

State of Rhode Island Tourism Site
www.visitrhodeisland.com

NOTE ABOUT THE AUTHOR

ANN MARIE MARSHALL

Ann Marie Marshall (née Harrington), one of nine children of John Dennis and Anna Marie (Flood) Harrington of East Providence, is a native Rhode Islander. She is a proud "Townie," and mother of three grown children.

She is a Real Estate agent with Phillips Post Road Realty and a business consultant. She helps people rent and purchase property in Rhode Island. She is a longtime business advocate for her hometown of North Kingstown and nearby Exeter.

She writes a weekly real estate blog:
MyRhodeIslandHome.wordpress.com

Ann Marie has been a national advocate for entrepreneurs and micro-business owners for more than 25 years. She has helped entrepreneurs start numerous small businesses, acquire millions of dollars in commercial loans, and taught business workshops to thousands of business owners at conferences and workshops in the U.S. and Eastern Europe. After traveling more than a million miles, she loves Rhode Island best!

Ann Marie was the Republican candidate in 2008 and 2010 for Rhode Island State Representative in District 31 to serve the citizens of North Kingstown and Exeter.

What's Next! for Rhode Island continues at:
http://WhyRIMatters.blogspot.com

www.ingramcontent.com/pod-product-compliance
Lightning Source LLC
Chambersburg PA
CBHW021145020426
42331CB00005B/911